Tolerance

Kimberley Jane Pryor

 **Marshall Cavendish**
Benchmark
New York

This edition first published in 2009 in the United States of America by Marshall Cavendish Benchmark.

Marshall Cavendish Benchmark
99 White Plains Road
Tarrytown, NY 10591
www.marshallcavendish.us

First published in 2008 by
MACMILLAN EDUCATION AUSTRALIA PTY LTD
15–19 Claremont St, South Yarra 3141

Visit our Web site at www.macmillan.com.au or go directly to www.macmillanlibrary.com.au

Associated companies and representatives throughout the world.

Library of Congress Cataloging-in-Publication Data

Pryor, Kimberley Jane.
  Tolerance / by Kimberley Jane Pryor.
    p. cm. — (Values)
  Includes index.
  ISBN 978-0-7614-3129-9
  1. Toleration—Juvenile literature. 2. Children—Conduct of life—Juvenile literature. I. Title.
  BJ1431.P79 2008
179'.9—dc22

                                    2008001672

Edited by Helena Newton
Text and cover design by Christine Deering
Page layout by Raul Diche and Domenic Lauricella
Photo research by Naomi Parker and Legend Images

Printed in the United States

Acknowledgments
The author and the publisher are grateful to the following for permission to reproduce copyright material:

Front cover photograph of grandparent learning to use a computer © Greg Nicholas/iStockphoto.com

Photos courtesy of:
BananaStock Royalty-Free, **15**; BrandX Pictures, **3**, **16**, **29**; Digital Vision/Getty Images, **19**, **22**, **25**; PictureIndia RF/Getty Images, **26**; Stockbyte/Getty Images, **13**; © Lisa Eastman/iStockphoto.com, **24**; © Sheryl Griffin/iStockphoto.com, **9**; © bonnie jacobs/iStockphoto.com, **30**; © lilly3/iStockphoto.com, **23**; © Sean Locke/iStockphoto.com, **11**; © marmion/iStockphoto.com, **20**; © Linda & Colin McKie/iStockphoto.com, **8**; © Greg Nicholas/iStockphoto.com, **1**, **10**; © Cheryl Paquin/iStockphoto.com, **28**; © Glenda Powers/iStockphoto.com, **7**; © Daniela Andreea Spyropoulos/iStockphoto.com, **21**; © Josef Vital/iStockphoto.com, **18**; Photodisc, **4**, **14**; Photos.com, **17**; © Rodolfo Arpia/Shutterstock.com, **5**; © Galina Barskaya/Shutterstock.com, **12**; © Muriel Lasure/Shutterstock.com, **6**; © Alfred Wekelo/Shutterstock.com, **27**.

While every care has been taken to trace and acknowledge copyright, the publisher tenders their apologies for any accidental infringement where copyright has proved untraceable. Where the attempt has been unsuccessful, the publisher welcomes information that would redress the situation.

For Nick, Ashley and Thomas

1 3 5 6 4 2

Contents

Glossary words

When a word is printed in **bold**, you can look up its meaning in the Glossary on page 31.

Values

Values are the things you believe in. They guide the way:

- you think
- you speak
- you **behave**

Values help you to play fairly with your friends on a slide.

Values help you to decide what is right and what is wrong. They also help you to live your life in a **meaningful** way.

Values help you to follow the rules of hopscotch.

Tolerance

Tolerance is being aware that people are different from one another. It is knowing that each person is **unique**.

Even identical twins are different from one another.

Tolerance is also understanding that different people have different **opinions** and **beliefs**. It is accepting that different people do things in different ways.

Some people believe that mice make good pets and others do not.

Tolerant People

Tolerant people **appreciate** differences. They accept other people the way they are and do not try to change them.

Traditional clothing worn in India is different from clothing worn in other countries.

Tolerant people know that others have feelings and needs. They are understanding toward their family, friends, and neighbors.

A parent shows understanding when his or her child is upset.

Being Tolerant of Family

Families are made up of people of different ages. Younger people show tolerance when they teach older people new things.

Children try to be tolerant when they teach older family members how to use computers.

Parents are usually tolerant of their children. They do not mind if their children take time to learn something new.

Parents know it takes time for young children to learn how to help in the yard.

Being Tolerant of Friends

Tolerant people accept that their friends may have different interests. They understand that friends may enjoy different sports and hobbies.

You may have a friend who plays a musical instrument.

You can show tolerance by forgiving your friends when they make mistakes. This shows your friends that you like them, even though they are not perfect.

Friends stick together, even when one has made a mistake.

Being Tolerant of Neighbors

Tolerant people welcome new neighbors to their street. They make them feel included by being friendly and helpful.

Inviting new neighbors to play in the park will make them feel welcome.

People with disabilities may live in your neighborhood. They are the same as other people, but may have special needs.

These friends have a neighbor in a wheelchair.

Ways To Be Tolerant

There are many different ways to be tolerant toward your family, friends, and neighbors. Being aware of other people is a good way to start being tolerant.

One way of being tolerant is to take turns on the swing.

Good ways to practice tolerance are to include and to learn from others. Being patient is also a part of being tolerant.

These children wait patiently to be picked up after school.

17

Being Aware of Others

Being aware of others is a sign of tolerance. Tolerant people are aware that each person is an individual. This means that no two people in the world are the same.

Older family members can teach young people new things.

Tolerant people are aware of other people's feelings and beliefs. They do not say things that will hurt or **offend** others.

You need to be careful not to upset your classmates when giving a talk.

Respecting Different Kinds of Families

Respecting different kinds of families shows tolerance and understanding. Not all families live in the same kinds of homes and neighborhoods.

This girl lives with her grandparents, not with her parents.

Many families follow a **religion**. Each religion has different beliefs. These beliefs help people to live a meaningful life.

People with different beliefs can play together if everyone shows tolerance.

Accepting Other Cultures

Accepting people from other **cultures** is a way of showing tolerance. People from other cultures may have different beliefs and **customs**.

The Samburu people of Kenya, Africa, have their own beliefs and customs.

Tolerant people accept that others may speak a different language. They enjoy listening to **traditional** music and watching traditional dances.

Many Chinese people celebrate Chinese New Year with a traditional dragon parade.

Including Others

Including others in activities is a way of being tolerant. If tolerant people belong to a group, they do not leave others out on purpose. They invite them to join in.

A friend who is left out
may feel sad and lonely.

Choosing different people to work with on projects shows tolerance. Tolerant people do not always work with the same people. They do not mind if they work with girls or boys.

These boys and girls are working happily as a group on a project.

Learning from Others

When you visit other people, you learn about their way of life. People from other countries may eat foods you have never seen before.

You can learn about Indian food if you share a meal with an Indian family at home.

Tolerant people enjoy finding out how other people do things. They enjoy learning how other people arrange their homes and gardens.

Japanese gardens often have beautiful stepping-stone paths over water.

Being Patient

Being patient is a part of being tolerant. Some people are very patient. They accept that some things take a long time to happen.

Patient people accept that small plants take time to grow.

Patient people stay calm while they are waiting for something or someone. They understand that they cannot have what they want right away.

Waiting in line without complaining shows patience.

Personal Set of Values

There are many different values. Everyone has a personal set of values. This set of values guides people in big and little ways in their daily lives.

Tolerance helps teachers to be patient when students are learning new things.

Glossary

appreciate   are grateful for

behave   act in a certain way

beliefs   things that people believe and accept as true

cultures   skills, arts, beliefs, customs, and language that groups of people share

customs   the typical ways that people do things

meaningful   important or valuable

offend   insult someone or hurt their feelings

opinions   things you think or decide

religion   a set of beliefs about God, or gods and how to worship God, or gods

traditional   something that has been done in the same way for a very long time

unique   one of a kind

Index